THE NATIVE AMERICAN INDIAN APPROVED MEANS TO GATHER FOOD

US History 6th Grade

Children's American History

Speedy Publishing LLC

40 E. Main St. #1156

Newark, DE 19711

www.speedypublishing.com

Copyright 2017

The Native American Indians historically would obtain their food by farming, gathering, fishing and hunting. In this book, you will be learning about how they were able to provide food on the table for their tribes.

HOW DID THEY GET THEIR FOOD?

Depending on the area they lived in and the tribe they were a part of, Native Americans would get their food by varying methods that included farming, gathering, fishing and hunting. Most of the tribe would use a combination of these methods to obtain food, however, several would focus on a certain area such as hunting or farming.

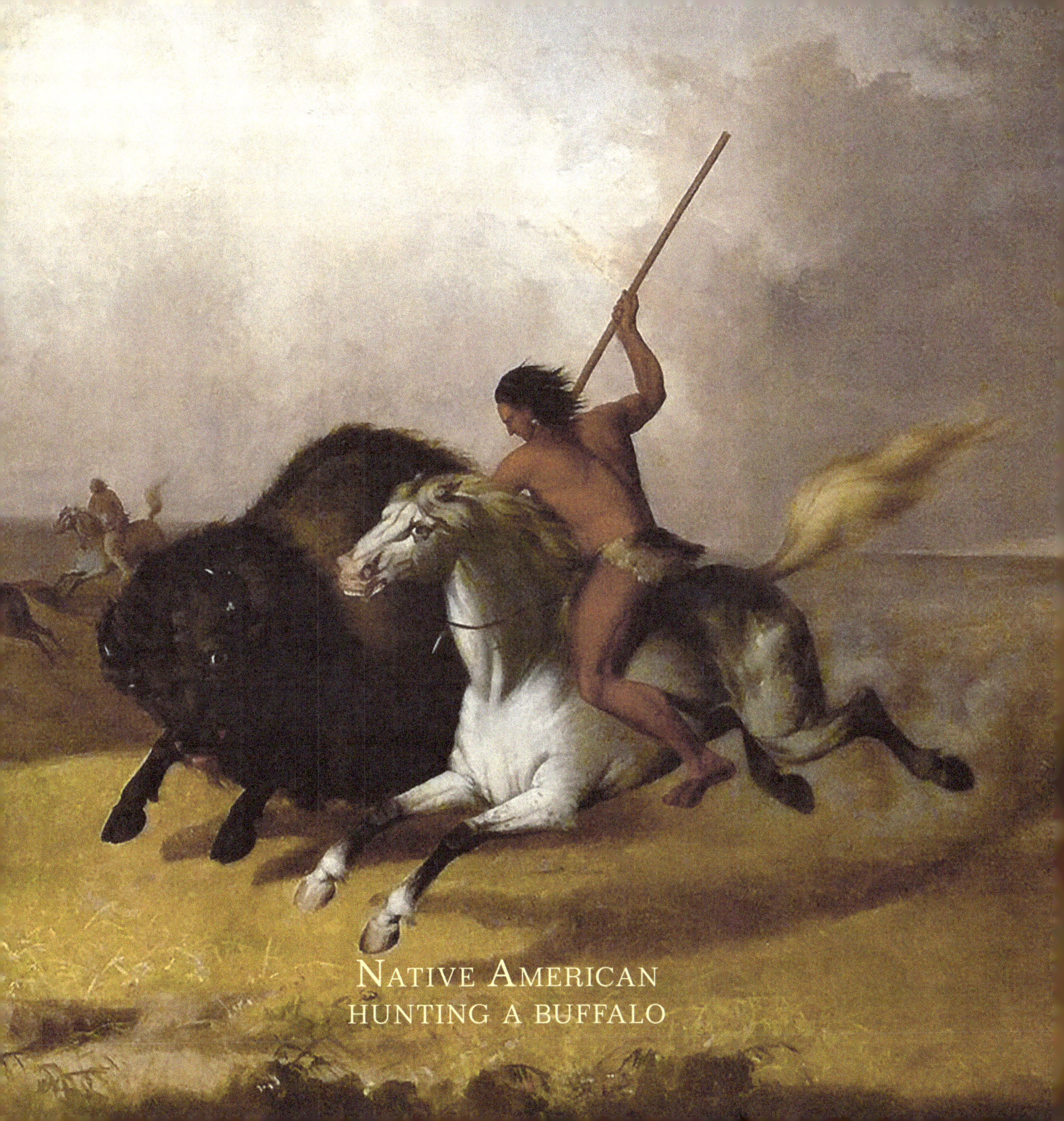

NATIVE AMERICAN
HUNTING A BUFFALO

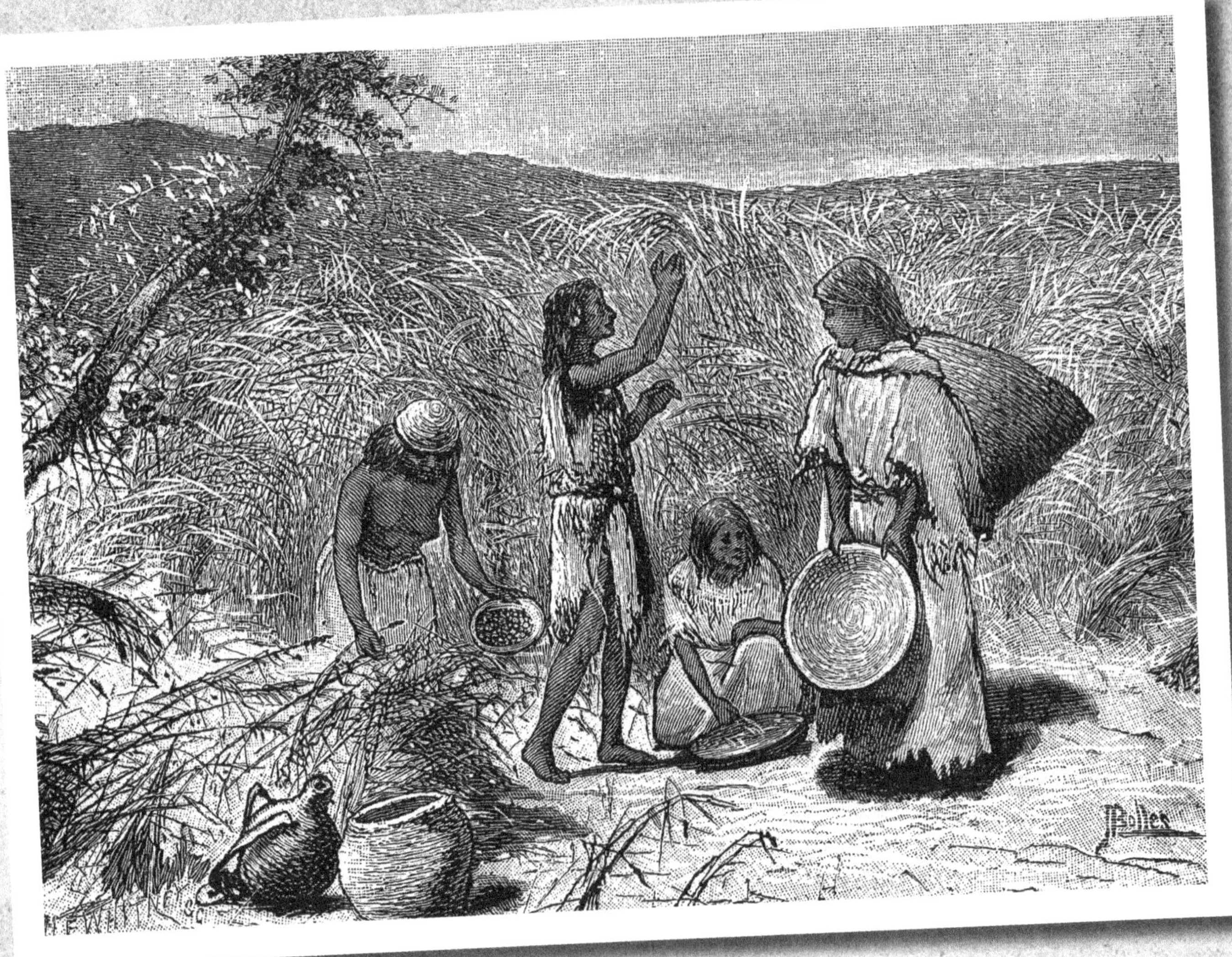

NATIVE AMERICAN
HUNTING A BUFFALO

FARMING

Several of the American Indian tribes would grow crops for food, however the farming experts would tend to be in the southern states such as the Southwest and Southeast.

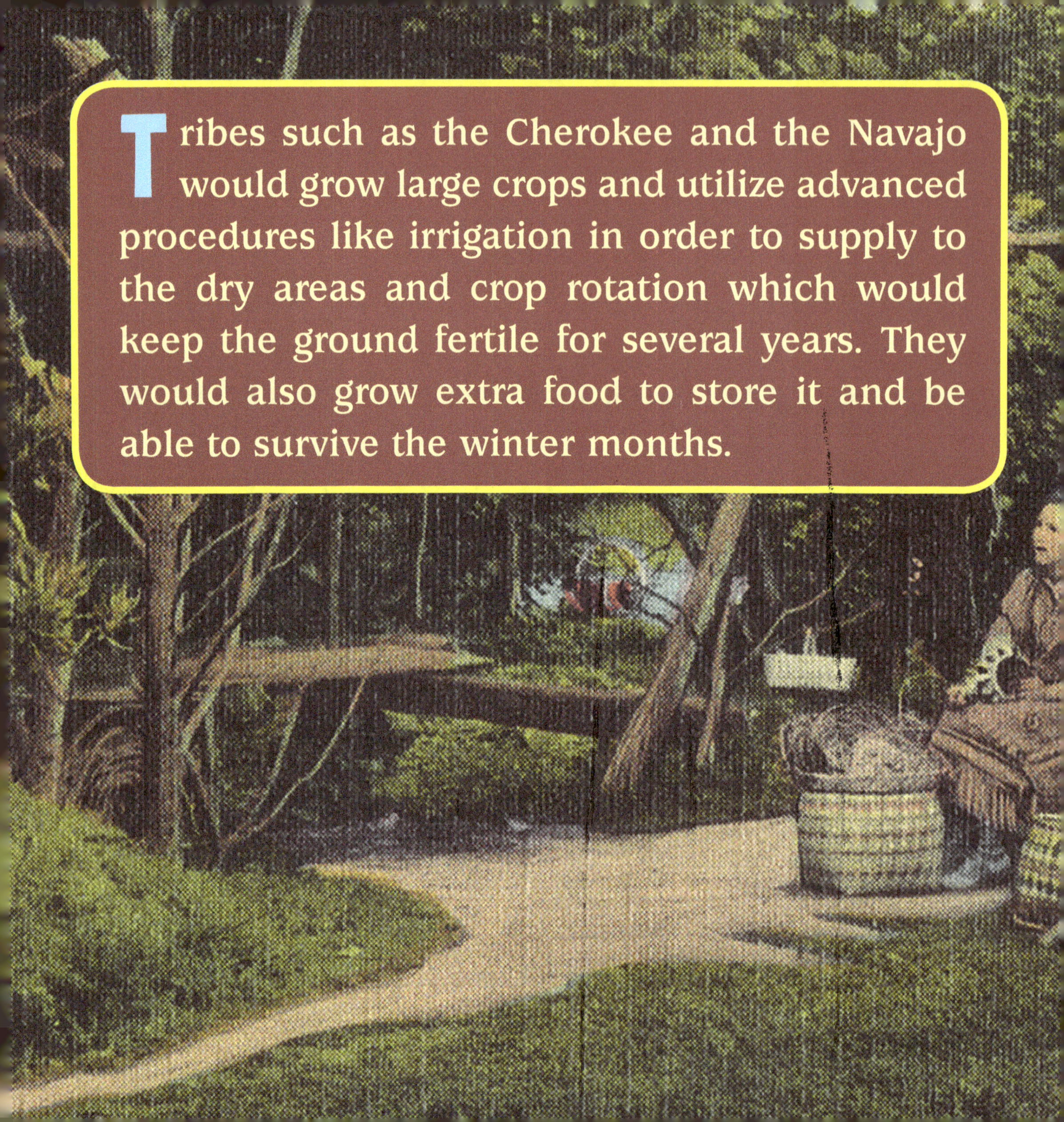

Tribes such as the Cherokee and the Navajo would grow large crops and utilize advanced procedures like irrigation in order to supply to the dry areas and crop rotation which would keep the ground fertile for several years. They would also grow extra food to store it and be able to survive the winter months.

VARIEGATED MAIZE

Corn, which they referred to as maize, was the main crop of the Native American peoples. Many of the tribes would eat maize since it was easy to store during the winter and could be ground into flour. It was eaten almost daily by several tribes and became a major part of American Indian culture.

They were able to utilize all of it, using the cob for fuel in fires and the husks were used for crafts. While maize was the main crop, several other crops the tribes cultivated were potatoes, cotton, pumpkins, squash and beans.

THANKSGIVING GATHERING

GATHERING

When people obtain food from their environment, it is referred to as gathering. The Native American tribes gathered foods including nuts, berries, or other fruits produced from naturally growing berry bushes and trees. Many of the Native American peoples used gathering to obtain some of their food.

HUNTING AND FISHING

Several tribes obtained most of their food by hunting, which was a major part of the Native American culture.

FISHING WITH THE USE OF SPEARS

FISHING

Tribes living near large lakes or in coastal areas specialized in fishing. They would often use nets or spears to catch fish, which was smoked or dried and stored for the winter months. Native Americans living in the north would ice fish, by cutting a hole in the ice and the using spears to catch the fish.

BUFFALO OR BISON

In the Great Plains area, they relied greatly on buffalo, also known as bison. They not only ate it for food, but also used much of it for other aspects of their lives. The bones were used for tools.

BUFFALO HUNT

The hides would be used for clothes, blankets, and for making the covers for their teepees. They would make rope from the bison's hair and use their tendons as thread for sewing. Most all parts of the bison were utilized.

The bison is a large and powerful animal that travels in large herds. To be able to hunt them, the American Indians would need to work together and be clever. Often, they would get them to stampede into a pit or off of a cliff.

OTHER ANIMALS

The Native American Indians that lived in other parts of the country would hunt using weapons like the bow and arrow or use traps and snares for hunting rabbits, ducks, deer and other such animals.

AMERICAN BISON

THE AMERICAN BISON

Native to North American, the American Bison is considered a bovine. Originally, they covered a lot of the open land located east of the Appalachians Mountains from Mexico up to Canada. Before the arrival of the Europeans, massive herds had roamed these plains, with an estimate of more than 30 million American bison at one time.

HOW LARGE ARE BISON?

Surprisingly, they are quite large, being North America's largest animal on land. The males are bigger than the females, growing over 11 feet long, 6 feet tall, and weighing more than 2000 pounds – that's more than a ton!

They have a brown coat that gets long and shaggy in the winter to keep them warm. It then gets lighter in the summer so they won't get too hot. Bison have a big forequarters and head as well as a hump on their back right behind

their head. They have two horns that grow up to about 2 feet long, which they use for fighting and defense among the herds. The females and males both grow horns.

WHAT DO THEY EAT?

Bison are known as herbivores, which means they eat plants. They mostly graze on the plants that grow in the prairies, such as sedges and grasses. Most of their day is spent grazing and they spend the rest of their time resting and chewing their cud. They then travel to another spot and go through the same process again.

Bison can be very dangerous, so don't let their docile actions fool you. They are unpredictable and wild and if provoked, they will attack. Never get too close to a wild bison as they can be deadly.

ARE BISON BIG AND SLOW?

The answer is yes and no. While they are huge, they are still very fast. They actually can run faster than a horse and are able to jump more than six feet high. So, don't believe that you can run faster than a bison if it has decided to attack.... you will not be able to.

ARE THEY CONSIDERED TO BE ENDANGERED?

The bison were hunted by the thousands during the 1800s. Estimates state that as many as 100,000 were killed every day. Typically, they were hunted for their skins to be used as coats. They became almost extinct by the late 1800s. That left only a few hundred from the millions that had once roamed the lands.

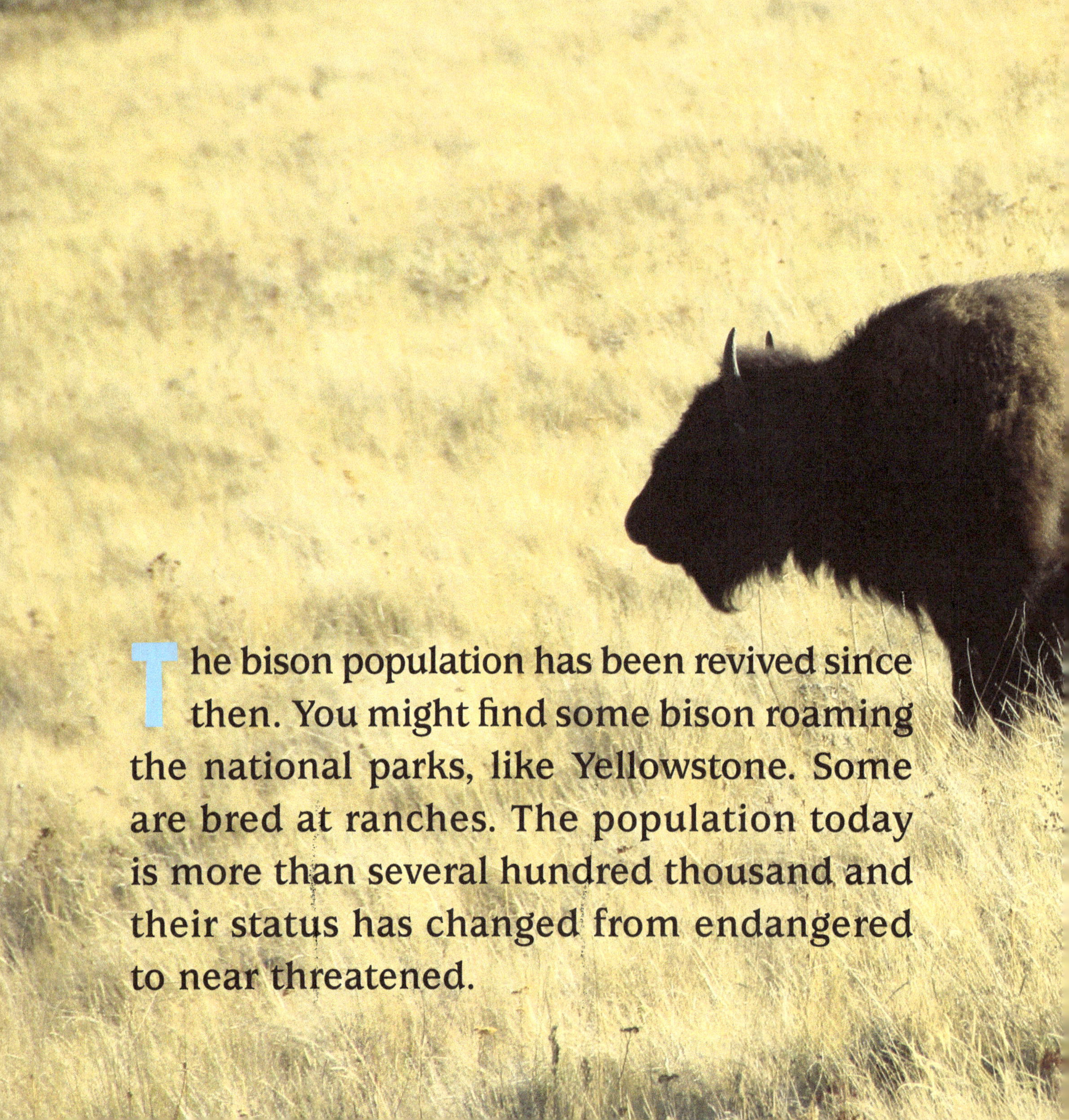

The bison population has been revived since then. You might find some bison roaming the national parks, like Yellowstone. Some are bred at ranches. The population today is more than several hundred thousand and their status has changed from endangered to near threatened.

WHAT WERE SOME TYPICAL NATIVE AMERICAN FOODS?

As discussed early, maize was the most important Native American Indian food crop. Most of their tribes grew some corn, and tribes that didn't would trade for it. Other examples of their crops included squash, beans, pumpkins, wild rice, sunflowers, potatoes, tomatoes, sweet potatoes, peanuts, peppers, papayas, and avocados.

M ost tribes ate meat-heavy diets, whether they farmed or not. Some of their favorites meats included elk, buffalo, rabbit, deer and caribou; salmon and other types of fish; geese, turkeys, ducks and other birds; clams and other species of shellfish and marine animals such as seals and even whales.

Almost any animal was occasionally added to the menu, animals you might not think of eating, such as monkeys, snakes or porcupines. Many tribes had strong beliefs against letting food go to waste, so if an animal was killed for another reason, they would go ahead and try to eat it.

They also enjoyed some foods found naturally including honey, eggs, maple syrup and sugar, nuts (including pine nuts, peanuts, cashews, acorn and hickory nuts), fruit (including strawberries, cranberries, raspberries, blueberries, wild plums, chokecherries and persimmons), as well as a variety of roots, greens and beans.

THE ARRIVAL OF EUROPEANS

HOW DID THE ARRIVAL OF THE EUROPEANS AFFECT THEIR EATING HABITS?

When the Europeans arrived, they introduced new animals and plants that did not originally exist in the Americas, including cows, bananas, sheep and wheat.

Some of the farming tribes, including the Navajos or the Mexican Indian tribes, started raising these new farm animals and crops in addition to the corn or whatever other traditional crops they were already farming. Many Native Americans in those tribes still farm today and have been farming these "new" foods for centuries.

Once the Europeans took over, some tribes had to change a lot of their traditional lifestyles. Once the Europeans had killed off most of the bison, tribes that had previously

followed the bison herds had to figure out
new ways to live. Some of the tribes now raise
buffalo on their ranches.

Most of the jungles and forests have been cleared which makes it more difficult to make a living by hunting. In some of the rural areas of Alaska, Canada and South America, some Native Americans and Intuit (Eskimo) are still are able make a living by trapping and hunting, but it has become rarer. One of the greatest changes was the Indian tribes being forced to relocate to reservations which were far from their original homelands.

AN ESKIMO GIRL FISHING

In several cases, they had to give up their previous way of life in this new location since the environment was not the same and the land was not good for their type of agriculture.

Some of their recipes and foods are enjoyed today by the Native American people. However, other than a few remote tribes in the rainforest, Native Americans enjoy modern food.

For additional information about Native American Tribes and how they obtained food for dinner, you can go to your local library, research the internet, and ask questions of your teachers, family and friends.

Visit
BABY PROFESSOR
EDUCATION KIDS
www.BabyProfessorBooks.com
to download Free Baby Professor eBooks
and view our catalog of new and exciting
Children's Books